MEALS FOR ME AND YOU

MEALS FOR ME AND YOU

COLLINS & BROWN

The Good Housekeeping website is
www.goodhousekeeping.co.uk

ISBN 978-1-909397-56-9

A catalogue record for this book is available from
the British Library.

Reproduction by Mission Productions Ltd,
Hong Kong
Printed and bound by 1010 Printing International Ltd,
China

This book can be ordered direct from the publisher.
Contact the marketing department, but try your
bookshop first.

www.anovabooks.com

NOTES

Both metric and imperial measures are given for
the recipes. Follow either set of measures, not a
mixture of both, as they are not interchangeable.

All spoon measures are level.
1 tsp = 5ml spoon; 1 tbsp = 15ml spoon.

Ovens and grills must be preheated to the specified
temperature.

Medium eggs should be used except where
otherwise specified. Free-range eggs are
recommended.

Note that some recipes contain raw or lightly
cooked eggs. The young, elderly, pregnant women
and anyone with an immune-deficiency disease
should avoid these because of the slight risk of
salmonella.

Contents

Simple Suppers for One

Perfect Eggs

Follow these tried and tested steps for perfect baked eggs and omelettes.

Baking

You can crack eggs into individual dishes or into a large shallow pan and bake them. They may be cooked on their own, or baked with vegetable accompaniments.

1 Generously smear individual baking dishes or one large baking dish with butter.

2 Put in any accompaniments, if using (see Variations and accompaniments, opposite). If using vegetable-based accompaniments, use the back of a spoon to make a hollow in which to break each egg. Crack the egg or eggs into the hollows.

3 Bake for 8–10 minutes at 200°C (180°C fan oven) mark 6, or 15–18 minutes at 180°C (160°C fan oven) mark 4 until the whites are set; the yolks should still be quite runny.

2

3

Variations and accompaniments

Eggs are delicious baked on a simple bed of sautéed vegetables (such as ratatouille), lightly browned diced potatoes with onions, and also on well-cooked spinach.

Accompaniments must be fully cooked before they are transferred to the dish and the raw eggs put on top. Other simple additions include freshly chopped herbs. If you like, drizzle a small spoonful of cream and a good grinding of ground black pepper on top of the eggs before baking.

Perfect omelettes

❏ Don't add butter until the pan is already hot, otherwise it will brown too much
❏ Beat the eggs lightly
❏ Use a high heat

Classic omelette

1 To make an omelette for one person, heat a heavy-based 18cm (7in) frying pan or omelette pan. Using a fork, beat 2 eggs and season with salt and freshly ground black pepper.

2 Add 15g (½oz) butter to the pan and let it sizzle for a few moments without browning, then pour in the eggs and stir a few times with a fork.

3 As the omelette begins to stick at the sides, lift it up and allow the uncooked egg to run into the gap.

4 When the omelette is nearly set and the underneath is brown, loosen the edges and give the pan a sharp shake to slide the omelette across.

5 Add a filling (such as grated cheese or fried mushrooms), if you like, and fold the far side of the omelette towards you. Tilt the pan to slide the omelette on to the plate and serve.

Gruyère and Watercress Omelette

Hands-on time: 5 minutes
Cooking time: 5 minutes

½ tbsp vegetable oil
2–3 large eggs, lightly beaten and seasoned (depending on hunger!)
a small handful of roughly chopped watercress
25g (1oz) grated Gruyère cheese
salt and freshly ground black pepper
green salad and crusty bread to serve

1 Heat the oil over a low heat in a small frying pan. Add the beaten eggs and use a spatula to move them around the pan for 30 seconds.
2 Next, top the egg with the watercress and cheese.
3 Continue cooking until the base of the omelette is golden (check with the spatula) and the cheese is melting. Fold in half and serve with a green salad and crusty bread.

Serves 1

Deluxe Baked Eggs

Hands-on time: 5 minutes
Cooking time: about 12 minutes

15g (½oz) butter
100g (3½oz) sliced chestnut
  mushrooms
1 tbsp brandy (optional)
leaves from 1 fresh thyme sprig
rocket leaves
2 medium eggs
salt and freshly ground black pepper

1 Preheat the grill. Heat the butter over a high heat in a small frying pan, then cook the mushrooms for 5 minutes or until tender. Add the brandy, if you like, and the thyme leaves and cook for 1 minute, then season well and put to one side.

2 Next, put some rocket leaves in the bottom of a shallow, individual ovenproof serving dish, then top with the mushroom mixture. Crack in the eggs, garnish with a few more thyme leaves and season.

3 Grill for 5 minutes or until the eggs are set. Serve immediately.

SAVE TIME

To get ahead, prepare the mushroom mixture in step 1 up to 2 hours in advance. Keep at room temperature. Complete steps 2 and 3 to finish the recipe.

Serves 1

Poached Haddock and Egg

Hands-on time: 10 minutes
Cooking time: 10 minutes

150g (5oz) smoked haddock fillet
200ml (7fl oz) full-fat milk
½ tsp plain flour
50ml (2fl oz) double cream
1 medium egg
a handful of freshly chopped chives
freshly ground black pepper
boiled new potatoes and seasonal
   vegetables to serve

1 Bring a small, deep pan of water to the boil. Meanwhile, put the haddock into a small frying pan, skin-side down, and pour the milk over it. If the fish isn't covered, top up with water.

2 Bring the milk to the boil, then reduce the heat and simmer gently for 4 minutes or until the fish is just cooked (it should flake when pushed with a knife). Carefully lift the fish out, putting the milk to one side, then discard the skin and put the fillet on a plate. Cover with foil to keep warm.

3 Discard all but about 100ml (3½fl oz) of the cooking milk and put the pan and milk back on to the heat. Whisk in the flour and add the cream. Simmer, stirring occasionally, to thicken.

4 Meanwhile, break the egg into a cup, then tip it gently into boiling water. Simmer the egg for 2–3 minutes, using a metal spoon to baste the top with a little of the hot water, until the white is set but the yolk is still soft (test by carefully lifting the egg out of the water with a slotted spoon and pushing gently with your finger). Lift the egg out of the water with a slotted spoon and drain on kitchen paper.

5 To serve, strain the sauce over the fish, top with the egg and sprinkle with some ground black pepper and chopped chives. Serve with boiled new potatoes and seasonal vegetables.

Serves 1

Crusted Cod with Grilled Tomatoes

Hands-on time: 10 minutes
Cooking time: about 10 minutes

2 tsp olive oil

150g (5oz) boneless fillet of cod

about 25g (1oz) white bread (stale bread is ideal)

1 tbsp freshly chopped parsley or 1 tsp dried mixed herbs

finely grated zest of ¼ lemon

about 75g (3oz) bunch of cherry tomatoes on the vine

boiled new potatoes or salad to serve

1 Preheat the grill. Heat 1 tsp of the oil in a small grill-proof frying pan on the hob. Fry the cod, skin-side down, in the pan for 3 minutes.

2 Meanwhile, coarsely grate the bread or whiz it in a food processor to make crumbs. Put the crumbs into a bowl with the parsley or mixed herbs, the lemon zest and the remaining oil. Carefully lift the part-cooked fish on to a baking sheet and top with the breadcrumb mixture.

3 Put the tomatoes on the vine next to the cod and grill for 5 minutes or until the fish is cooked and the tomatoes have just burst. Serve with boiled new potatoes or salad.

Serves 1

Marinated Feta

Hands-on time: 5 minutes, plus marinating (optional)

½ × 200g (7oz) pack feta

1½ tbsp extra virgin olive oil

1 tbsp each freshly chopped dill and mint

grated zest of ¼ orange

salt and freshly ground black pepper

salad and crusty bread to serve

1 Put the feta into a bowl (trying not to break it) and pour the oil over.

2 Scatter the dill, mint and orange zest over it, then season to taste with salt and ground black pepper. Cover and leave to marinate for 1 hour, if you have time.

3 Serve with salad and crusty bread.

Aromatic Griddled Veggies

Hand-on time: 5 minutes
Cooking time: about 10 minutes

a few slices of aubergine and
courgette, cut lengthways
olive oil to brush
1 tsp extra virgin olive oil
1 tsp green peppercorns
1 tsp capers
1 tsp freshly chopped rosemary
mozzarella cheese (optional)
salt and freshly ground black pepper

1 Heat a griddle pan over a high heat. Brush the vegetable slices with olive oil and griddle on both sides (turning once rather than repeatedly flipping) until tender and nicely charred.
2 Arrange on a plate and drizzle with the extra virgin olive oil, then scatter on the peppercorns, capers and rosemary. Season, then dot over a few torn pieces of mozzarella, if you like.

SAVE TIME

To get ahead, complete the recipe to the end of step 1 up to 1 hour in advance. Put the vegetables on to the plate and drizzle with the oil. Cover loosely. To serve at room temperature, complete the recipe. To serve warm, reheat on the plate in an oven preheated to 180°C (160°C fan oven) mark 4 for 10 minutes, then complete the recipe.

Serves 1

The Well-stocked Fridge and Freezer

Having the right equipment can make life so much easier in the kitchen. Consider the space you have available: do you have room for a separate fridge and freezer? Choose wisely to ensure you get the most out of what you can fit in your kitchen.

The perfect fridge

The fridge is vital for any kitchen and keeps food fresh for longer. However, it is the main culprit for waste. The bigger it is, the more it becomes a repository for out-of-date condiments and bags of wilted salad leaves that lurk in its depths.

Safe storage:

- ❑ Cool cooked food to room temperature before putting in the fridge
- ❑ Wrap or cover all food except fruit and vegetables
- ❑ Practise good fridge discipline: the coldest shelves are at the bottom so store raw meat, fish and poultry there

To make sure the fridge works properly

- ❑ Don't overfill it
- ❑ Don't put hot foods in it
- ❑ Don't open the door more than you need to
- ❑ Clean it regularly

The perfect freezer

This is an invaluable storage tool and if you use it properly – particularly with batch cooking – you can save time and avoid wastage. Make sure you allow food time to thaw: if you leave it overnight in the fridge, your meal will be ready to pop into the oven when you get home from work. You can have all sorts of standbys waiting for you: breads, cakes, pastry, frozen vegetables and fruit such as raspberries and blackberries, cream, stocks, soups, herbs and bacon.

How to store food:
- ❑ Freeze food as soon as possible after purchase
- ❑ Label cooked food with the date and name of the dish
- ❑ Freeze food in portions
- ❑ Never put warm foods into the freezer, wait until they have cooled
- ❑ Check the manufacturer's instructions for freezing times
- ❑ Don't refreeze food once it's thawed

What not to store in the freezer:
- ❑ Whole eggs – freeze whites and yolks separately
- ❑ Fried foods – they lose their crispness and can go soggy
- ❑ Some vegetables – cucumber, lettuce and celery have too high a water content
- ❑ Some sauces – mayonnaise and similar sauces will separate when thawed

To make sure the freezer works properly:
- ❑ Defrost it regularly
- ❑ Keep the freezer as full as possible

Thawing and reheating food:
- ❑ Some foods, such as vegetables, soups and sauces, can be cooked from frozen – dropped into boiling water, or heated gently in a pan until thawed
- ❑ Ensure other foods are thoroughly thawed before cooking
- ❑ Cook food as soon as possible after thawing
- ❑ Ensure the food is piping hot all the way through after cooking

Dine Alone
and Love It

Dine Alone and Love It!

Whether you live alone or just need to feed yourself on an evening when the family is out, cooking for one can present challenges. But with a little practice, some helpful hints and inspiring recipes, the rewards of dining solo are plentiful.

Learn to love your freezer

A freezer is a handy companion, whether you're cooking for one or for 20. Leftovers, buy-one-get-one-frees and bulk-freezing all play their part. Label and date all entries clearly in freezer-safe bags or containers, and portion things appropriately before you freeze.

Shop sensibly

Luckily, shopping for one is easier now than ever. At a butcher or fishmonger, there's no problem in asking for smaller portions, and more supermarkets are also stocking individual portions of meat and fish. Try to self-select fruit and vegetables rather than buying big bags that end up spoiling.

Storecupboard success

A key to speedy, wallet-friendly and healthy meals is a well-stocked cupboard. Keep a reserve of dried pasta, lentils, noodles and rice, canned (or carton) tomatoes and pulses, tomato purée, soy sauce, stock and dried herbs and spices.

Planning is key

It's not always easy to plan meals in advance, but it does help. If you know you'll be using half an aubergine in one recipe, pick another recipe to use up the rest.

Double up

Batch cooking and freezing the extra saves time and money. When you next have a free hour or two, make some favourite meals that freeze well. Then when you're too tired to cook, you can simply thaw your dinner.

Save the veg

Buying fresh produce for one can be tricky, as it's easy to get carried away. Most veg (if bought in peak condition), whole or not, will keep for up to five days in the fridge if tied in polythene bags with a few holes pricked into them.

Cook building blocks

Over the weekend (or whenever you have time) cook a larger quantity of a staple meat that can be used for different meals throughout the week. So, if you roast four chicken breasts (on the bone gives great flavour) on a Sunday afternoon, you could have roast on Sunday evening, chicken curry on Monday, a chicken salad on Tuesday and chilli chicken on Wednesday.

Practice makes perfect

Be experimental. Set yourself a goal to try a certain number of new recipes, techniques or ingredients each month. You'll learn new skills, stop food boredom creeping in and bolster your repertoire.

Get it on file

An up-to-date folder of favourite recipes helps with shopping and ensures you eat a variety of foods and nutrients. So next time you rustle up a dish you enjoy, keep or copy the recipe for your file.

Be size savvy

Next time you cook a staple such as rice or lentils, note the raw weight and whether you ate all of the cooked result. That way, you can keep a record (tape a chart inside a cupboard door) so you don't over- or under-cater.

Treat yourself

One of the joys of cooking for one is that you don't need to cater to someone else's palate, and you can have treats. If you like your scrambled eggs covered in sweet chilli sauce or prefer lamb to beef, that's fine.

Do the maths

Most savoury recipes are easily divisible into portions (or you can make the larger quantity and freeze it). It's trickier to adjust a baking recipe: the exact quantity of ingredients has to be delicately balanced.

Make it fast

Quick-cook methods such as grilling, frying and hot roasting are perfect for solo cooks – and deliver fantastic flavour, too.

Wrap it up

Cooking in a parcel is great for single servings. Put a portion of meat or fish on a large square of foil or baking parchment, add thinly sliced veg and aromatics (garlic, ginger, chilli, fresh herbs, and so on), fold up the edges and pour in a little water or stock. Seal, then cook in the oven, or steam.

No more tears

Next time you shop, buy a few extra white onions. Peel and chop finely, then freeze in a freezer bag (laid as flat as possible). Next time a recipe calls for a little onion, use your frozen stash.

Cracked it

An egg is already packaged as a single serving, and two eggs count as a portion of protein. Store eggs in their carton in the fridge to stop them taking on taints from other foods. To check if eggs are edible beyond their best-before date, carefully slide into a bowl of water. The eggs are fine if they sink, but bin them if they float.

Sweet tooth

Most cookie dough freezes well – divide into smaller portions so that you can bake a few at a time. With cakes, choose a recipe that freezes (baked cheesecakes are ideal). Cool completely, slice and separate with baking parchment. Wrap and freeze. Then you can take out a slice to thaw, rewrap and freeze the rest.

Speedy Lamb Stew

Hands-on time: 5 minutes
Cooking time: about 25 minutes

150g (5oz) lamb loin fillet, cut into
   2.5cm (1in) cubes

1 tsp plain flour

1 tsp oil

½ tsp ground cinnamon

15g (½oz) roughly chopped blanched
   almonds

25g (1oz) roughly chopped dried
   apricots

½ × 400g can chopped tomatoes

40g (1½oz) couscous

salt and freshly ground black pepper

fresh coriander to garnish

1 Dust the lamb cubes with the flour. Heat the oil in a small pan over a medium heat and fry the lamb until well browned. Stir in the cinnamon, almonds and apricots. Pour in the tomatoes and add enough water to just cover the meat, then simmer gently for 15 minutes.

2 Meanwhile, put the couscous into a bowl and just cover with boiling water. Cover with clingfilm and leave for 10 minutes.

3 When the stew is ready, check the seasoning and fluff up the couscous with a fork. Serve the couscous with the lamb, garnished with coriander.

Serves 1

Steak Sandwich

Hands-on time: 5 minutes
Cooking time: about 6 minutes, plus resting

200g (7oz) rump steak

1 tbsp extra virgin olive oil, plus extra to drizzle

1 bread roll, such as ciabatta, cut in half horizontally

a handful of rocket or spinach leaves

Parmesan or blue cheese

salt and freshly ground black pepper

1 Pat the steak dry with kitchen paper and season well. Heat the oil in a frying pan over a high heat and fry the steak for 2–3 minutes on each side for medium (cook for shorter/longer if you prefer). Put the steak on a board, cover with foil and leave to rest for 5 minutes.

2 Meanwhile, toast the bread, cut-side down, in the empty steak pan for 1 minute.

3 Put half the toasted bread on a plate, top with the steak slices and a handful of rocket or spinach leaves. Shave some Parmesan over, or, alternatively, crumble on some blue cheese. Drizzle with some more oil and top with the remaining bread.

Serves 1

Perfect Fish

These techniques are suitable for flat-shaped fish such as turbot, plaice and sole. Flat fish is often used filleted for recipes and sometimes rolled around a stuffing. For this, it also needs to be skinned.

Cleaning and skinning

1 To gut, slit open the skin just behind the head of the fish where the stomach sac begins. Work your fingers in and pull the entrails out, then snip out the remainder with scissors.
2 Thick-skinned fish, such as sole, can be skinned by hand. Make a nick right down to the backbone where the body meets the tail. Work your fingers under the skin until you have lifted enough to get a grip on.
3 Holding the tail in one hand, pull on the flap in the direction of the head. The skin should come away in a single sheet.

2
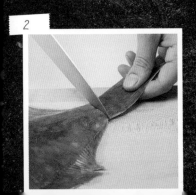

3

1. **Thinner skinned fish** can be filleted first, then skinned using a knife. Put the fillet on a board with the skin down and the tail towards you. Make a nick in the tail flesh, just deep enough to cut through to the skin, and lift the little flap of flesh with the knife.
2. Hold the knife on the skin at a very shallow angle, almost parallel to the worksurface, and work it between flesh and skin to remove the skin in a single piece.

Filleting

1. Insert a sharp knife between the flesh and ribs on one side of the backbone. Holding the knife nearly parallel to the backbone, cut between the backbone and the flesh until detached.
2. Turn the fish round and repeat on the other side. Smaller fish may only provide two fillets.

Herby Buttered Sole with Sweet Potato Wedges

Hands-on time: 10 minutes
Cooking time: about 30 minutes

1 medium sweet potato, unpeeled, cut into thick wedges

1 tbsp sunflower oil

¼ tsp dried thyme

3 tbsp plain flour

150g (5oz) skinless sole or plaice fillets (see page 34 or ask your fishmonger to skin the fish for you)

15g (½oz) butter

1 tbsp soft green fresh herbs, such as parsley and sage, finely chopped

2 tsp capers

salt and freshly ground black pepper

crisp green salad and lemon wedges to serve (optional)

1 Preheat the oven to 200°C (180°C fan oven) mark 6. Put the sweet potato wedges on a baking tray, sprinkle with 1 tsp of the oil, the thyme and plenty of seasoning and toss through. Cook in the oven for 30 minutes, turning occasionally until golden and tender.

2 About 5 minutes before the end of the cooking time, put the flour on a lipped plate and add some seasoning, then lay the fish fillets in the flour to lightly coat (tap off any excess). Heat the remaining oil over a high heat in a large non-stick frying pan. Fry the fish fillets for 2 minutes, turning halfway through the cooking time, until lightly golden and opaque.

3 Lift the fish out on to a plate and keep warm. Take the empty fish pan off the heat and add the butter, fresh herbs and capers. Stir until melted.

4 Pour the hot butter mixture over the fish and serve with the sweet potato wedges and a crisp green salad and lemon wedges, if you like.

Serves 1

Goat's Cheese Puff

Hands-on time: 15 minutes
Cooking time: about 25 minutes

50g (2oz) trimmed green beans
¼ × 375g puff pastry block
plain flour to dust
40g (1½oz) soft goat's cheese
1 tbsp freshly chopped mint
beaten egg to glaze
salt and freshly ground black pepper

1 Bring a pan of water to the boil, then add the beans and cook for 3 minutes. Drain, then plunge them into a bowl of ice-cold water. Drain again and pat dry.

2 Preheat the oven to 200°C (180°C fan oven) mark 6. Roll out the pastry on a floured worksurface to make a rough 12.5cm (5in) square. Put the pastry square on a baking sheet.

3 Put the goat's cheese, mint and seasoning to taste in a small bowl and stir to combine. Spread the cheese mixture in a strip diagonally across the pastry, then lay the beans on top of the cheese in a neat bundle. Brush the visible pastry with beaten egg, then fold the two opposite corners over the beans to enclose. Brush the pastry with egg and bake for 15–20 minutes until golden. Serve immediately.

SAVE TIME

To get ahead, make the puff and glaze with the egg (do not cook) up to 2 hours in advance. Chill. Complete the recipe to serve.

Serves 1

Oriental Baked Tofu

Hands-on time: 10 minutes
Cooking time: 15 minutes

150g (5oz) regular tofu
½ garlic clove, thinly sliced
2cm (¾in) piece fresh root ginger,
    peeled and cut into matchsticks
1 tsp soy sauce
freshly ground black pepper
a small handful of fresh coriander
a few chilli rings
lime wedges to serve

1 Preheat the oven to 220°C (200°C fan oven) mark 7. Stack two 30.5cm (12in) sheets of greaseproof paper, baking parchment or foil on top of each other and put the tofu on one side.

2 Sprinkle the garlic slices, ginger, soy sauce and some ground black pepper over the tofu. Fold the paper/parchment/foil over, then fold in the edges to seal. Put the parcel on a baking sheet and cook for 15 minutes. Open the parcel and sprinkle in a small handful of fresh coriander and a few chilli rings. Serve with lime wedges.

SAVE TIME

To get ahead, assemble the parcel and put on a tray up to 3 hours in advance. Chill. Complete the recipe to serve.

Serves 1

Butter Bean Masala

Hands-on time: about 10 minutes
Cooking time: about 10 minutes

½ tbsp vegetable oil

1 shallot, sliced

1 garlic clove, crushed

1 tsp garam masala

¼–½ red chilli (depending on taste –
  freeze the remainder to use at a later
  date), seeded and finely chopped

2 tomatoes, roughly chopped

410g can butter beans, drained and
  rinsed

a handful of fresh coriander or
  spinach, chopped

salt and freshly ground black pepper

1 Heat the oil in a pan, add the shallot and gently cook for 5 minutes. Stir in the garlic, garam masala and chilli and cook for 1 minute, then add the tomatoes and 100ml (3½fl oz) water. Simmer for 3 minutes, occasionally squashing the tomatoes with a wooden spoon.

2 Stir in the butterbeans and heat through. Stir through the coriander or spinach and check the seasoning. Serve immediately.

Serves 1

Simple Suppers
for Two

Take 5 Quick Salad Dressings

Blue Cheese

To make 100ml (3½fl oz), you will need: 50g (2oz) Roquefort cheese, 2 tbsp low-fat natural yogurt, 1 tbsp white wine vinegar, 5 tbsp extra virgin olive oil, salt and freshly ground black pepper.

1 Crumble the cheese into a food processor and add the yogurt, vinegar and oil. Whiz for 1 minute or until thoroughly combined. Season to taste with salt and ground black pepper.

2 If not using immediately, store in a cool place and use within one day.

Chilli Lime

To make 125ml (4fl oz), you will need: ¼ red chilli, seeded and finely chopped, 1 garlic clove, crushed, 1cm (½in) piece fresh root ginger, peeled and finely grated, juice of 1½ large limes, 50ml (2fl oz) olive oil, 1½ tbsp light muscovado sugar, 2 tbsp fresh coriander leaves, 2 tbsp fresh mint leaves.

1 Put the chilli, garlic, ginger, lime juice, oil and sugar into a food processor or blender and whiz for 10 seconds to combine. Add the coriander and mint leaves and whiz together for 5 seconds to chop roughly.

2 If not using immediately, store in a cool place and use within two days.

Mustard

To make about 100ml (3½fl oz), you will need: 1 tbsp wholegrain mustard, juice of ½ lemon, 6 tbsp extra virgin olive oil, salt and freshly ground black pepper.

1 Put the mustard, lemon juice and oil into a small bowl and whisk together. Season to taste with salt and ground black pepper.

2 If not using immediately, store in a cool place and whisk briefly before using.

Lemon and Parsley

To make about 100ml (3½fl oz), you will need: juice of ½ lemon, 6 tbsp extra virgin olive oil, 4 tbsp freshly chopped flat-leafed parsley, salt and freshly ground black pepper.

1 Put the lemon juice, oil and parsley into a medium bowl and whisk together. Season to taste with salt and ground black pepper.

2 If not using immediately, store in a cool place and whisk briefly before using.

Mint Yogurt

To make about 175ml (6fl oz), you will need: 150g (5oz) Greek yogurt, 3-4 tbsp freshly chopped mint leaves, 2 tbsp extra virgin olive oil, salt and freshly ground black pepper.

1 Put the yogurt into a bowl and add the mint and oil. Season to taste with salt and ground black pepper.

2 If not using immediately, store in a cool place and use within one day.

Crunchy Chicken Salad

Hands-on time: 20 minutes
Cooking time: about 15 minutes, plus cooling

2 × 125g (4oz) skinless chicken breasts
1 large carrot
75g (3oz) sugarsnap peas
1 red pepper, seeded
½ mango, peeled and stoned
a large handful of fresh coriander,
    roughly chopped
15g (½oz) salted peanuts, roughly
    chopped, to garnish

For the dressing
zest and juice of 1 lime
¾ tbsp toasted sesame oil
1 tbsp honey
1 tsp fish sauce
¾ tsp sesame seeds
salt and freshly ground black pepper

1 Put the chicken breasts into a pan and cover with cold water. Bring to the boil, then reduce the heat and simmer gently for 15 minutes. Take off the heat and put to one side for 10 minutes.

2 Meanwhile, cut the carrot, sugarsnap peas, red pepper and mango into thin strips. Put the veg into a large bowl and stir in the mango.

3 Combine the dressing ingredients with some salt and ground black pepper in a small bowl.

4 Lift the chicken out of the water and, when cool enough to handle, shred. Add to the vegetable bowl with the dressing and coriander and toss through. Garnish with peanuts and serve.

Serves 2

Broad Bean and Feta Salad

Hands-on time: 10 minutes
Cooking time: 5 minutes

225g (8oz) podded broad beans
100g (3½oz) feta, chopped
2 tbsp freshly chopped mint
2 tbsp extra virgin olive oil
a squeeze of lemon juice
salt and freshly ground black pepper
lemon wedges to serve (optional)

1 Cook the beans in lightly salted boiling water for 3–5 minutes until tender. Drain, then plunge them into cold water and drain again. Remove their skins, if you like.

2 Tip the beans into a bowl, add the feta, mint, oil and a squeeze of lemon juice. Season well with salt and ground black pepper and toss together. Serve with lemon wedges, if you like.

Serves 2

Greek Pasta Salad

Hands-on time: 10 minutes
Cooking time: 20 minutes

3 tbsp olive oil
2 tbsp lemon juice
150g (5oz) cooked pasta shapes,
   cooled
75g (3oz) feta, crumbled
3 tomatoes, roughly chopped
2 tbsp small pitted black olives
½ cucumber, roughly chopped
1 small red onion, finely sliced
salt and freshly ground black pepper
freshly chopped parsley and lemon
   zest to garnish
crusty bread to serve

1 Mix the oil and lemon juice together
   in a salad bowl, then add the pasta,
   feta, tomatoes, olives, cucumber
   and onion. Season to taste with
   salt and ground black pepper, then
   stir to mix.
2 Garnish with parsley and lemon zest
   and serve with crusty bread.

Serves 2

Croque Monsieur

Hands-on time: 5 minutes
Cooking time: 8 minutes

4 slices white bread

butter, softened, to spread, plus extra for frying

Dijon mustard, to taste

125g (4oz) Gruyère cheese

4 slices ham

1 Spread each slice of bread on both sides with the butter. Then spread one side of two slices of bread with a little Dijon mustard.

2 Divide the cheese and ham between the two mustard-spread bread slices. Top each with the remaining bread and press down.

3 Heat a griddle with a little butter until hot and fry the sandwiches for 2–3 minutes on each side until golden and crispy and the cheese starts to melt. Slice in half and serve immediately.

Serves 2

Scotch Woodcock

Hands-on time: 5 minutes
Cooking time: 5 minutes

2 large slices wholemeal bread
butter
Gentleman's Relish or anchovy paste
  to spread
4–6 tbsp milk
2 medium eggs
a pinch of cayenne pepper
50g can anchovies, drained

1 Toast the bread, remove the crusts and spread with butter. Cut in half and spread with Gentleman's Relish or anchovy paste.
2 Melt a knob of butter in a pan. Whisk together the milk, eggs and cayenne pepper, then pour into the pan and stir slowly over a gentle heat until the mixture begins to thicken. Take off the heat and stir until creamy.
3 Divide the mixture between the anchovy toasts and top with thin strips of anchovy fillet, arranged in a criss-cross pattern.

Omelette Arnold Bennett

Hands-on time: 15 minutes
Cooking time: about 20 minutes

125g (4oz) smoked haddock
50g (2oz) butter
150ml (¼ pint) double or single cream
3 medium eggs, separated
50g (2oz) Cheddar, grated
salt and freshly ground black pepper
rocket salad to serve

1 Put the fish in a pan and cover with water. Bring to the boil, then reduce the heat and simmer gently for 10 minutes. Drain and flake the fish, discarding the skin and bones.

2 Put the fish in a pan with half the butter and 2 tbsp of the cream. Toss over a high heat until the butter melts. Leave to cool.

3 Preheat the grill. Beat the egg yolks with 1 tbsp of the cream and some seasoning. Stir in the fish mixture. Put the egg whites into a clean, grease-free bowl and whisk until they form stiff peaks, then fold into the yolks.

4 Heat the remaining butter in an omelette pan. Fry the egg mixture, but make sure it remains fairly fluid. Do not fold over. Slide it on to a flameproof serving dish.

5 Blend together the cheese and remaining cream, then spread on top of the omelette and brown under the grill. Serve immediately with a rocket salad.

Serves 2

Baked Eggs with Spinach and Mushrooms

Hands-on time: 10 minutes
Cooking time: 15 minutes

2 tbsp olive oil
125g (4oz) mushrooms, chopped
225g (8oz) fresh spinach
2 medium eggs
2 tbsp single cream
salt and freshly ground black pepper

1 Preheat the oven to 200°C (180°C fan oven) mark 6. Heat the oil in a large frying pan, add the mushrooms and stir-fry for 30 seconds. Add the spinach and stir-fry until wilted. Season to taste, then divide the mixture between two shallow ovenproof dishes.

2 Carefully break an egg into the centre of each dish, then spoon 1 tbsp single cream over it.

3 Cook in the oven for about 12 minutes until just set – the eggs will continue to cook a little once they're out of the oven. Grind a little more black pepper over the top, if you like, and serve.

Serves 2

Quick Fish and Chips

Hands-on time: 15 minutes
Cooking time: 12 minutes

4 litres (7 pints) sunflower oil to
  deep-fry

125g (4oz) self-raising flour

¼ tsp baking powder

¼ tsp salt

1 medium egg

150ml (¼ pint) sparkling
  mineral water

2 hake fillets (weight about
  125g/4oz each)

450g (1lb) Desiree potatoes, cut into
  1cm (½in) chips

salt, vinegar and mayonnaise
  to serve

1 Heat the oil in a deep-fryer to 190°C
   (test by frying a small cube of bread
   – it should brown in 20 seconds).

2 Whiz the flour, baking powder, salt,
   egg and water in a food processor
   or blender until combined into a
   batter. Remove the blade from the
   food processor. (Alternatively, put
   the ingredients into a bowl and beat
   everything together until smooth.)
   Drop one of the fish fillets into the
   batter to coat it.

3 Put half the chips into the deep-
   fryer, then add the battered fish. Fry
   for 6 minutes or until just cooked,
   then remove and drain well on
   kitchen paper. Keep warm if not
   serving immediately.

4 Drop the remaining fillet into the
   batter to coat, then repeat step 3
   with the remaining chips. Serve
   with salt, vinegar and mayonnaise.

Serves 2

Toad in the Hole

Hands-on time: 10 minutes
Cooking time: about 30 minutes

125g (4oz) plain flour, sifted
2 large eggs, lightly beaten
150ml (¼ pint) semi-skimmed milk
2 tbsp oil
4 pork sausages
salt and freshly ground black pepper
steamed carrots and broccoli or green
   beans to serve

1 Preheat the oven to 220°C (200°C fan oven) mark 7. Put the flour into a bowl, make a well in the centre and pour in the eggs and milk. Whisk the batter thoroughly and season it well with salt and ground black pepper.

2 Divide the oil and sausages between two 600ml (1 pint) shallow ovenproof dishes and cook in the oven for 10 minutes, turning once or twice.

3 Divide the batter between the dishes and continue to cook for 15–20 minutes until the batter is puffy and a rich golden colour all over. Serve immediately, with steamed carrots and broccoli or green beans.

Serves 2

Four-cheese Gnocchi

Hands-on time: 3 minutes
Cooking time: 10 minutes

350g pack fresh gnocchi
300g tub fresh four-cheese sauce
240g pack sunblush tomatoes
2 tbsp freshly torn basil leaves, plus
  basil sprigs to garnish
1 tbsp freshly grated Parmesan
15g (½oz) butter, chopped
salt and freshly ground black pepper
salad to serve

1 Cook the gnocchi in a large pan of lightly salted boiling water according to the pack instructions or until all the gnocchi have floated to the surface. Drain well and put the gnocchi back into the pan.

2 Preheat the grill. Add the four-cheese sauce and tomatoes to the gnocchi and heat gently, stirring, for 2 minutes.

3 Season with salt and ground black pepper, then add the basil and stir again. Spoon into individual heatproof bowls, sprinkle a little Parmesan over each one and dot with butter.

4 Cook under the grill for 3–5 minutes until golden and bubbling. Garnish the gnocchi with basil sprigs and serve with salad.

Serves 2

Naan Pizza

Hands-on time: 5 minutes
Cooking time: about 10 minutes

2 plain naans
2 tbsp caramelised red onion chutney
50g (2oz) soft goat's cheese, crumbled
75g (3oz) cherry tomatoes, quartered
2 fresh thyme sprigs, leaves picked
a small handful of rocket
extra virgin olive oil to drizzle
   (optional)
freshly ground black pepper
green salad to serve

1 Preheat the oven to 220°C (200°C fan oven) mark 7. Put the naans on a baking sheet, then spread the onion chutney over them. Dot with the goat's cheese, tomatoes and thyme leaves, then season with ground black pepper.
2 Cook in the oven for 5–10 minutes until the cheese has softened and the pizza is piping hot. Garnish with rocket leaves, drizzle with oil, if you like, and serve with a green salad.

Serves 2

Perfect Stir-fry

Stir-fries can be as simple or as substantial as you feel like making them. And if you buy ready-prepared stir-fry vegetables, a meal can be on the table in minutes. Ensure your wok or pan is very hot before you start cooking and keep the ingredients moving.

Stir-frying vegetables

Stir-frying is perfect for non-starchy vegetables, as the quick cooking preserves their colour, freshness and texture.

1. Cut the vegetables into even-size pieces. Heat some vegetable oil in a large wok or frying pan until smoking-hot. Add crushed garlic to taste and cook for a few seconds, then remove and put to one side.
2. Add the vegetables to the wok and toss and stir them. Keep them moving constantly as they cook.
3. When the vegetables are just tender, but still with a slight bite, turn off the heat. Put the garlic back into the wok and stir well. Add soy sauce and sesame oil to taste, toss and serve on warmed plates.

2

Stir-frying fish

Choose a firm fish such as monkfish, as more delicate fish will break up.

1 Cut the fish into bite-size pieces. Heat a wok or large pan until very hot and add oil to coat the inside.
2 Add the fish and toss over a high heat for 2 minutes until just cooked. Remove to a bowl.
3 Cook the other ingredients you are using for the stir-fry. Put the fish back into the wok or pan for 1 minute to heat through, then serve immediately.

3

Stir-frying tips:

❑ Cut everything into small pieces of uniform size so that they cook quickly and evenly

❑ If you're cooking onions or garlic with the vegetables, don't keep them over the high heat for too long or they will burn

❑ Add liquids towards the end of cooking so that they don't evaporate

Stir-fried Salmon and Broccoli

Hands-on time: 10 minutes
Cooking time: about 6 minutes

2 tsp sesame oil
1 red pepper, seeded and thinly sliced
½ red chilli, thinly sliced
1 garlic clove, crushed
125g (4oz) broccoli florets
2 spring onions, sliced
2 salmon fillets, about 125g (4oz) each,
   cut into strips
1 tsp Thai fish sauce
2 tsp soy sauce
wholewheat noodles to serve

1 Heat the oil in a wok or large frying pan and add the red pepper, chilli, garlic, broccoli florets and spring onions. Stir-fry over a high heat for 3–4 minutes.

2 Add the salmon, fish sauce and soy sauce and cook for 2 minutes, stirring gently. Serve immediately with wholewheat noodles.

Serves 2

Five-minute Stir-fry

Hands-on time: 2 minutes
Cooking time: 5 minutes

1 tbsp sesame oil

175g (6oz) raw peeled tiger prawns, deveined (see page 82)

50ml (2fl oz) ready-made sweet chilli and ginger sauce

225g (8oz) ready-prepared mixed stir-fry vegetables, such as sliced courgettes, broccoli and green beans

1 Heat the oil in a large wok or frying pan, add the prawns and sweet chilli and ginger sauce and stir-fry for 2 minutes.

2 Add the mixed vegetables and stir-fry for a further 2–3 minutes until the prawns are cooked and the vegetables are heated through. Serve immediately.

Serves 2

Dining for Two

Warm Bacon Salad

Hands-on time: 10 minutes
Cooking time: about 15 minutes

4 handfuls of soft salad leaves
1 small red onion, thinly sliced
75g (3oz) cubed pancetta
1 thick slice white bread, diced
2 medium eggs
25g (1oz) Parmesan, pared into
  shavings with a vegetable peeler
fresh flat-leafed parsley sprigs to
  garnish

For the dressing
1 tbsp Dijon mustard
2 tbsp red wine vinegar
2 tbsp fruity olive oil
salt and freshly ground black pepper

1 Put the salad leaves and onion into
  a large bowl. Fry the pancetta in a
  non-stick frying pan until it begins
  to release some fat. Add the diced
  bread and continue to fry until the
  pancetta is golden and crisp.
2 Whisk all the dressing ingredients
  together in a small bowl with
  some seasoning.

3 Half-fill a small pan with cold water
  and bring to the boil. Turn the heat
  right down – there should be just a
  few bubbles on the bottom of the
  pan. Break the eggs into a cup, then
  tip them gently into the pan and
  cook for 3–4 minutes, using a metal
  spoon to baste the tops with a little
  of the hot water. Lift the eggs out of
  the water with a slotted spoon and
  drain on kitchen paper.
4 Tip the pancetta, bread and any pan
  juices over the salad leaves. Add the
  Parmesan, then pour the dressing
  over the salad. Toss well, then divide
  between two plates. Top each with
  an egg, season to taste, then garnish
  with parsley sprigs and serve.

Serves 2

Chicken Tarragon Burgers

Hands-on time: 30 minutes, plus chilling
Cooking time: 12 minutes

225g (8oz) minced chicken
2 shallots, finely chopped
1 tbsp freshly chopped tarragon
25g (1oz) fresh breadcrumbs
1 large egg yolk
oil to grease
salt and freshly ground black pepper
burger buns, mayonnaise or Greek
  yogurt, salad leaves and tomato
  salad to serve

1 Put the chicken in a bowl with the shallots, tarragon, breadcrumbs and egg yolk. Mix well, then beat in about 75ml (3fl oz) cold water and season with salt and ground black pepper.

2 Lightly oil a foil-lined baking sheet. Divide the chicken mixture into two portions and put on the foil. Using the back of a wet spoon, flatten each portion to a thickness of 2.5cm (1in). Cover and chill for 30 minutes.

3 Preheat the barbecue or grill. Cook the burgers for 5–6 minutes on each side until cooked through, then serve in a toasted burger bun with a dollop of mayonnaise or Greek yogurt, a few salad leaves and tomato salad.

Perfect Prawns

Prawns are ideal for stir-frying and quick braising, because they need very brief cooking, otherwise they will become rubbery in texture.

Peeling, deveining and butterflying

1. To peel prawns, pull off the head and put to one side. Using pointed scissors, cut through the soft shell on the belly side.
2. Prise the shell off, leaving the tail attached. (Add to the head; it can be used later for making stock.)
3. Using a small sharp knife, make a shallow cut along the length of the back of the prawn. Use the point of the knife to carefully remove and discard the black vein (intestinal tract) that runs along the back of the prawn.
4. To 'butterfly' the prawn, cut halfway through the flesh lengthways from the head end to the base of the tail, and open up the prawn.

Langoustines and crayfish

Related to the prawn, langoustines and crayfish can be peeled in the same way as prawns.

To extract the meat from langoustine claws, pull off the small pincer from the claws, then work with small scissors to cut open the main section all the way along its length. Split open and carefully pull out the flesh in a single piece.

To extract the meat from large crayfish claws, crack them open using a hammer or lobster cracker, then carefully remove the meat.

Also known as scampi, langoustines are at their best when just boiled or steamed, and then eaten from the shells. They can also be used in a shellfish soup.

Crayfish are sold either live or cooked. To cook, boil in court bouillon for 5–10 minutes. Remove from the stock and cool. Eat crayfish from the shell or in a soup.

King Prawn Thai-style Salad

Hands-on time: 10 minutes
Cooking time: 5 minutes

2-3 tbsp green curry paste
200g (7oz) raw king prawns, peeled
    and deveined (see page 82)
juice of ½ lime
2 large carrots and 1 cucumber, peeled
    into ribbons
100g (3½oz) fresh coconut, cubed
a small handful of fresh mint, chopped
salt and freshly ground black pepper
lime wedges to serve

1. Heat a large frying pan, then stir in the curry paste and 1-2 tbsp hot water to loosen the paste. Cook for 30 seconds. Add the prawns and cook for 2-3 minutes until pink and cooked through.
2. Toss the lime juice, carrots, cucumber, coconut and mint through the prawns. Check the seasoning and serve with lime wedges to squeeze over.

SAVE TIME

Many supermarkets sell packs of fresh coconut in the chilled fruit section.

Serves 2

Prawns Fried in Garlic

Hands-on time: 10 minutes
Cooking time: 5 minutes

50g (2oz) unsalted butter

2 tbsp olive oil

12 raw Dublin Bay prawns in
  their shells

3 garlic cloves, crushed

4 tbsp brandy

salt and ground black pepper

flat-leafed parsley sprigs to garnish

lemon wedges and crusty bread
  to serve

1 Heat the butter with the olive oil
  in a large heavy-based frying pan.

2 Add the prawns and garlic and fry
  over a high heat for about 5 minutes,
  tossing the prawns constantly, until
  the shells have turned pink.

3 Sprinkle the brandy over the prawns
  and let it bubble rapidly to reduce
  right down. Season with salt and
  pepper.

4 Serve immediately, garnished with
  parsley and with lemon wedges and
  plenty of crusty bread. Remember to
  provide everyone with finger bowls
  and napkins.

Serves 2

Perfect Crab

Always buy crabs from a reputable fishmonger or supermarket fresh fish counter with a high turnover of stock and prepare it within 24 hours.

1. Live crabs must be humanely killed before cooking. Put the crab into the freezer for 5 minutes, then on to a board, with the belly facing up. Take a large chef's knife and plunge it straight down into the crab's head, right between or just below the eyes.
2. Put the crab into a pan of boiling water and cook for 5 minutes per 450g (1lb), or steam for 8 minutes per 450g (1lb).
3. To serve whole, simply set on the table with crackers and crab picks for diners to use themselves.
4. To remove the cooked meat for a recipe, put the crab on a board, with the belly facing up. Twist off the legs and claws. Lift off and discard the 'apron' (tail) – long and pointed in a male, short and broad in a female.
5. Pull the body out of the shell and remove and discard the feathery gills and grey stomach sac. Cut the body into pieces and pick out the meat using your fingers and a crab pick or small knife. Scrape the brown meat from the shell, keeping it separate from the white meat. If there is roe in a female, keep that separate, too.
6. Crack the claws with the back of a large knife, and pull out the meat in a single piece or in large chunks.
7. Cut through the shells of the legs with scissors, then cut through the opposite side. Pull off the shell halves to expose the meat and remove.

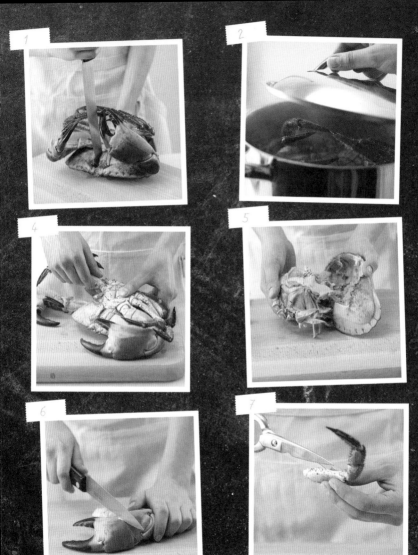

Crab and Orange Salad

🍴 **Hands-on time:** 20 minutes

2 small dressed crabs, each with about 100g (3½oz) crab meat
2 tsp freshly chopped flat-leafed parsley
buttered grilled focaccia slices and rocket leaves to serve

For the orange vinaigrette
grated zest and juice of 1 orange
½ tsp Dijon mustard
2 tsp wine vinegar
6 tbsp olive oil
salt and freshly ground black pepper

1 To make the vinaigrette, put the orange zest and 4 tbsp orange juice in a small bowl with the mustard, vinegar, salt and ground black pepper. Whisk together until thoroughly combined, then whisk in the oil.

2 Place the white crab meat in a small bowl and moisten with some of the vinaigrette; adjust the seasoning, if necessary.

3 Put a slice of grilled focaccia on each plate. Spread the brown crab meat on the bread if you like, then spoon the white meat mixture on top. Sprinkle with the parsley and a little extra vinaigrette. Serve with the rocket leaves.

SAVE EFFORT

Instead of fresh crab meat, use the same weight of frozen crab meat. Thaw at cool room temperature.

Classic Dressed Crab

Hands-on time: 30 minutes

1 medium cooked crab (weight about
   900g/2lb), cleaned (see page 88)
1 tbsp lemon juice
2 tbsp fresh white breadcrumbs
1 medium egg, hard-boiled
1 tbsp freshly chopped parsley
salt and freshly ground black pepper
salad leaves, and brown bread and
   butter to serve

1 Flake the white crab meat into a bowl, removing any shell or membrane, then add 1 tsp of the lemon juice and season with salt and ground black pepper to taste. Mix lightly with a fork.

2 Pound the brown crab meat in another bowl and work in the breadcrumbs and remaining lemon juice. Season to taste.

3 Using a small spoon, put the white crab meat into the cleaned crab shell, arranging it down either side and piling it up well. Spoon the brown meat into the middle between the sections of white meat.

4 Chop the egg white; press the yolk through a sieve. To garnish the crab, spoon lines of chopped parsley, sieved egg yolk and chopped egg white along the 'joins' between the white and brown crab meat. Serve on a bed of salad leaves, with brown bread and butter.

Serves 2

Red Mullet Baked in Paper

Hands-on time: 5 minutes
Cooking time: 30 minutes

2 red mullet (weight about
  225g/8oz each)
1 tbsp freshly chopped flat-leafed
  parsley
1 small onion, sliced
50g (2oz) mushrooms, chopped
finely grated zest and juice of 1 lemon
salt and freshly ground black pepper
boiled new potatoes and broccoli
  to serve

1 Preheat the oven to 180°C (160°C fan
  oven) mark 4. Cut two squares
  of greaseproof paper large enough
  to wrap the fish. Place the fish
  on top, then add the remaining
  ingredients. Fold the paper to make
  a secure parcel.

2 Place the parcels on a baking sheet
  and bake for 30 minutes or until
  the fish is tender. Serve the fish in
  their parcels with boiled potatoes
  and broccoli.

Teriyaki Tuna with Sesame Noodles

Hands-on time: 20 minutes, plus marinating
Cooking time: 10 minutes

2 tuna steaks

2 nests medium egg noodles

75g (3oz) green beans, trimmed and halved

1 tsp toasted sesame oil

4 spring onions, sliced

1 tbsp freshly chopped coriander

2 tsp sesame seeds

lime wedges to garnish

For the marinade

1 small garlic clove, crushed

2.5cm (1in) piece fresh root ginger, peeled and grated

3 tbsp teriyaki sauce

1 tbsp runny honey

1 tsp oil

1 Mix together the marinade ingredients in a non-metallic dish and add the tuna steaks. Leave to marinate in the fridge for 2 hours.

2 Preheat the grill to high. Cook the egg noodles according to the pack instructions with the green beans. Drain and cool under running water.

3 Meanwhile, put the tuna on a grill rack and cook for 3 minutes per side, brushing with the marinade, until firm but still moist.

4 Gently heat the sesame oil in a pan and toss in the noodles and green beans to reheat. Add the spring onions, coriander and sesame seeds.

5 To serve, divide the noodles between two plates, top with the tuna and garnish with lime wedges.

Serves 2

Pizza Fiorentina

Hands-on time: 25 minutes
Cooking time: about 45 minutes

125g (4oz) strong white flour, plus
   extra to dust

½ tsp fast-action (easy-blend)
   dried yeast

2 tbsp olive oil

1 onion, thinly sliced

75g (3oz) spinach leaves

2 tbsp tomato purée

½ tsp dried oregano

125g ball mozzarella, drained and torn
   into small pieces

2 large eggs

salt and freshly ground black pepper

1 Put the flour, yeast and ¼ tsp salt into a large bowl. Quickly mix in 75ml (3fl oz) warm water and ½ tbsp of the oil to make a soft, but not sticky, dough (add more flour/water as necessary). Tip on to a worksurface lightly dusted with flour and knead for 10 minutes. Form into a ball, then put back in the bowl, cover with clingfilm and leave to rise for 15 minutes.

2 Preheat the oven to 220°C (200°C fan oven) mark 7. Heat 1 tbsp of the remaining oil in a large frying pan, add the onion and gently cook for 15 minutes or until very soft. Add the spinach and cook for 2–3 minutes until wilted. Put to one side.

3 In a small bowl, stir together the tomato purée, oregano, remaining ½ tbsp oil and plenty of seasoning.

4 Flour a large baking tray. Roll out the dough on a lightly floured worksurface to make a rectangle roughly 20.5cm × 30.5cm (8in × 12in). Transfer to the prepared baking tray and cook in the oven for 5 minutes or until the base is just beginning to dry out. Take out of the oven and reduce the oven temperature to 180°C (160°C fan oven) mark 4.

5 Spread the tomato mixture over the dough, leaving a 2cm (¾in) border around the edge. Top with the mozzarella, followed by the onion mixture.

Serves 2

6 Crack an egg on to each half and season. Cook for a further 15–20 minutes until the pizza is golden and the eggs are cooked. Serve.

FREEZE AHEAD
To make ahead and freeze, prepare the pizza to the end of step 5 and cool completely. Open-freeze on the baking tray until solid, then wrap the pizza (off the tray) well in clingfilm and freeze for up to one month. To serve, unwrap and thaw on a baking tray, then warm the pizza for 5 minutes in the preheated oven before adding the eggs and completing the recipe.

One-pan Veggie Feast

Hands-on time: 5 minutes
Cooking time: 1 hour

750g (1lb 11oz) Jersey Royal potatoes
1 tbsp olive oil
a few fresh thyme sprigs
3 garlic cloves
½ lemon, cut into 4 wedges
25g (1oz) pitted sliced black olives
200g (7oz) cherry tomatoes on
  the vine
50g (2oz) vegetarian feta cheese,
  crumbled
salt and freshly ground black pepper
chopped fresh curly parsley to garnish

1 Preheat the oven to 190°C (170°C fan oven) mark 5. Put the potatoes into a roasting tin. Mix in the oil, thyme sprigs, garlic and lemon wedges and season. Roast in the oven for 45 minutes.

2 After 45 minutes, add the olives, cherry tomatoes and feta cheese and cook for a further 15 minutes or until the potatoes are tender.

3 Garnish with the parsley to serve.

Date Night

Melt-my-heart Camembert

Hands-on time: 5 minutes
Cooking time: about 20 minutes

250g wooden-boxed (stapled not glued) Camembert
1½ tbsp white wine or cider (optional)
2 fresh thyme sprigs, leaves only
salt and freshly ground black pepper

To serve
spears of steamed tenderstem broccoli
chunks of sourdough bread
rolls of ham
cornichons

1 Preheat the oven to 200°C (180°C fan oven) mark 6. Discard the lid of the Camembert box and any cloth wrapping. Take the cheese out of the box and unwrap, leaving it on the waxed paper. Slice off the top rind and discard. Put the cheese (on its paper), cut side up, back into the box and put on a baking sheet.

2 Season with salt and ground black pepper. Sprinkle the cheese with the alcohol, if you like, and half the thyme. Cook in the oven for 15–20 minutes until the cheese is golden on top and melted inside. Transfer the box to a board, garnish with the remaining thyme and serve with a choice of dippers.

Serves 2

Perfect Lobster

Sold either live, ready-cooked or ready-dressed, lobsters have a fine, delicate flavour. Serve with a simple accompaniment, such as good mayonnaise or a warm butter sauce. If you are able to buy a live lobster from your fishmonger, choose one that has all claws and legs intact.

1 To kill a lobster humanely before grilling, boiling or baking, put it into the freezer for 5 minutes. Then put it on a chopping board and hold the body firmly. Take a large chef's knife and plunge it straight down into the lobster's head, right between or just below the eyes. (It is inhumane to simply plunge it into boiling water or to put it into cold water and then bring it up to the boil.)

2 To cook the lobster whole, put it into a pan of boiling water. Boil steadily, allowing 10 minutes for the first 450g (1lb) and a further 5 minutes for each additional 450g (1lb). Leave to cool in the liquid.

3 If you are going to split the raw lobster for grilling or baking, cut the freshly killed lobster right through the head, then cut all the way down the length of the tail to split it in two.

4 Remove the head sac, which lies just behind the eyes, and discard. If you wish, you can remove the black coral (tomalley) and the green intestine, which lie inside the back of the shell just behind the head sac, or they may be left in place for cooking.

3

5 If you want the tail meat in one piece, split the head to where the tail begins, then use scissors to cut through the soft shell of the belly, down to the tail.

6 Pull the tail meat out with your fingers. Clean the head as in step 3. Cut off the claws and spiny legs. Crack the claws with a hammer or lobster cracker and remove the meat. Save the shells to make stock.

4

Lobster Thermidor

Hands-on time: 20 minutes
Cooking time: about 10 minutes

700g (1½lb) cooked whole lobster
150ml (¼ pint) double cream
1 tsp English mustard
40g (1½oz) butter
finely grated zest of ½ lemon
40g (1½oz) freshly grated Parmesan
1 tbsp freshly chopped chives, plus
   extra to garnish
salt and freshly ground black pepper
chunky thyme potato wedges and
   green salad to serve

1 Twist the claws off the lobster. Hit the heavy side of a claw sharply with the heel of a large knife, to embed the knife (keeping fingers well away). Now twist the knife until the claw cracks open. Pick the meat from the claw, taking care not to include the bone-like tendon, then roughly chop and put into a bowl. Repeat with the remaining claw.

2 Next, twist off the legs (they should be attached to a feathery gill, which you should discard). If you have time, crack the shell of the legs with a knife and ease out the meat with a toothpick – add the meat to the bowl. Now fully extend the lobster body in front of you (back facing up), lay on a board and push the tip of a large knife into the lobster just below the head. Now cut down the length of the back to halve the lobster. Ease out the white meat, roughly chop and add to the bowl.

Serves 2

Wash the halved shells and set on a baking tray.

3 Preheat the oven to 200°C (180°C fan oven) mark 6. Put the cream, mustard, butter and lemon zest into a medium pan. Heat gently, stirring, and simmer for 3–5 minutes until the mixture is the consistency of Greek yogurt. Stir in the lobster meat, Parmesan and most of the chives, then check the seasoning. Spoon the mixture back into the shells.

4 Cook for 5 minutes or until lightly golden and bubbling. Garnish with chives and serve with the potato wedges and a green salad.

Perfect Chocolate

Care must be taken when melting chocolate since it is an exacting process and determines the set appearance of the chocolate, giving it either a smooth glossy finish or a dull streaked appearance.

Melting chocolate

It is very important not to overheat any type of chocolate when melting it, as it will seize into an unusable mess.

The bowl in which you are melting the chocolate must also be clean and dry.

To melt chocolate over a pan

Break or chop the chocolate and put it into a heatproof bowl. Set the bowl over a pan of barely simmering water (making sure the bowl does not touch the water, but sits above it and that there is no space between the bowl and the pan rim). The steam from the water will gently melt the chocolate – stir occasionally to evenly distribute the heat and do not try to hurry the process along or else the chocolate might seize and become unworkable.

To melt chocolate in a microwave

Put the broken or chopped chocolate into a microwave-safe bowl. Microwave on full power for 1 minute. Stir, then heat again in 10-second bursts until the chocolate is smooth and melted. If the temperature of the chocolate gets too high, it can seize or will dry with a streaked surface.

Chocolate for dipping

This is ideal for small sweets, fruit and nuts. Strawberries are particularly good half-dipped in white chocolate. White chocolate is very versatile and may be used for all chocolate work. It also lends itself to being coloured. Use only powdered food colourings, as any liquid added to the chocolate will cause it to thicken and become unusable.

1 Fully immerse or half-coat your chosen item in melted chocolate. If needed, use a toothpick or a small fork to lift the item out of the chocolate, then shake to remove any excess.
2 Leave to set on a baking tray lined with baking parchment. Trim off any excess cooled chocolate, to neaten, and use.

Chocolate-dipped Strawberries

Hands-on time: about 10 minutes, plus chilling
Cooking time: 5 minutes

50g (2oz) white chocolate (or milk or plain, if you like), chopped
about 12 strawberries

1 Melt the chocolate in a heatproof bowl over a pan of gently simmering water (or blast for 20 seconds in the microwave until it is melted). Meanwhile, wash and thoroughly dry the strawberries, leaving the green hulls on.
2 Holding a strawberry by its hull, dip the fruit into the melted chocolate. Put on to a baking sheet lined with baking parchment. Repeat with each of the remaining berries, then chill to set. Serve the strawberries either chilled or at room temperature.

SAVE TIME

To get ahead, make these chocolate-dipped strawberries a day before and store, covered, in the fridge until needed.

Makes 12

Rosy Glow Cocktails

Hands-on time: 5 minutes

tiny fresh or dried rosebuds or some
  bright pink rose petals

½ tsp rosewater

pomegranate juice

sparkling white or rosé wine

1 If you have time, start by making some special ice cubes. Fill an ice cube tray with water, then drop in the fresh or dried rosebuds or rose petals. Freeze until solid.

2 Fill two tall glasses with the special rose or plain ice cubes, then add ¼ tsp rosewater to each glass. Half-fill the glasses with pomegranate juice, then top up with sparkling white or rosé wine and enjoy.

Serves 2

Sweet Treats

Luscious Lemon Pots

Hands-on time: 5 minutes, plus chilling (optional)

150g (5oz) condensed milk

50ml (2fl oz) double cream

grated zest and juice of 1 large lemon

1 passion fruit

1 Put the condensed milk, cream and lemon zest and juice into a medium bowl and whisk until thick and fluffy. Spoon into two small ramekins or coffee cups and chill until needed – or carry on with the recipe if you can't wait.

2 To serve, halve the passion fruit, scoop out the seeds and use to decorate the lemon pots.

Serves 2

Apple Compôte

Hands-on time: 10 minutes, plus chilling
Cooking time: 5 minutes

250g (9oz) cooking apples, peeled and chopped
juice of ½ lemon
1 tbsp golden caster sugar
ground cinnamon

To serve
25g (1oz) raisins
25g (1oz) chopped almonds
1 tbsp natural yogurt

1 Put the cooking apples into a pan with the lemon juice, sugar and 2 tbsp cold water. Cook gently for 5 minutes or until soft. Transfer to a bowl.
2 Sprinkle a little ground cinnamon over the top, cool and chill. It will keep for up to three days.
3 Serve with the raisins, chopped almonds and yogurt.

SAVE EFFORT

To microwave, put the apples, lemon juice, sugar and water into a microwave-safe bowl, cover loosely with clingfilm and cook on full power in an 850W microwave oven for 4 minutes or until the apples are just soft.

Serves 2

Boozy Pannacotta

Hands-on time: 10 minutes, plus soaking and chilling
Cooking time: 10 minutes

oil to grease
140ml (4½fl oz) double cream
150ml (¼ pint) semi-skimmed milk
3 tbsp light muscovado sugar
1 tbsp instant espresso coffee powder
50ml (2fl oz) Tia Maria or other
   coffee liqueur
40g (1½oz) plain chocolate (at least
   70% cocoa solids), chopped
1½ tsp powdered gelatine
1 tsp vanilla extract
2 chocolate-coated coffee beans
   (optional)

1 Oil two 150ml (¼ pint) individual pudding basins and line them with clingfilm. Pour 100ml (3½fl oz) of the cream into a small pan with the milk, sugar, coffee, 1 tbsp of the liqueur and the chocolate. Heat gently until the chocolate has melted, then bring to the boil.

2 Take the pan off the heat, sprinkle the gelatine over the surface and leave for 5 minutes. Stir well to ensure the gelatine is fully dissolved, then add the vanilla and mix well. Strain the mixture through a sieve into a jug, then pour into the lined basins and chill for 2 hours.

3 To serve, unmould the pannacottas on to plates and remove the clingfilm. Stir the rest of the liqueur into the remaining cream and drizzle around the pannacottas. Top with chocolate-coated coffee beans, if you like.

Tiramisu-for-you

🍴 **Hands-on time:** 5 minutes

50ml (2fl oz) cold espresso or strong black coffee

75g (3oz) full-fat mascarpone cheese

125ml (4fl oz) full-fat milk, chilled

1 tbsp almond-flavoured syrup or a few drops pure almond essence

1 tbsp maple syrup

1 tbsp whipped cream

½ tsp drinking chocolate powder

sponge fingers (boudoir biscuits) to serve

1 Pour the coffee into a blender and spoon in the mascarpone. Pour in the milk and add the almond syrup or essence and maple syrup.

2 Blend until smooth and well combined. Transfer to a glass cup and top with whipped cream.

3 Dust with drinking chocolate and serve with sponge fingers to dip.

Coffee Crème Brûlée

Hands-on time: 20 minutes
Cooking time: about 35 minutes, plus cooling and chilling

100ml (3½fl oz) double cream
100ml (3½fl oz) full-fat milk
1–1½ tbsp coffee liqueur
2 large egg yolks
25g (1oz) caster sugar
1 tbsp demerara sugar

1 Preheat the oven to 140°C (120°C fan oven) mark 1 and put a shallow ovenproof serving dish with roughly 400ml (14fl oz) capacity on a baking tray.

2 Heat the cream and milk together in a small pan until nearly boiling – there should be small bubbles around the edges of the liquid. Take the pan off the heat and mix in the coffee liqueur to taste.

3 Put the egg yolks and caster sugar into a medium heatproof bowl and stir until combined. Gradually mix in the hot cream mixture, then strain into a jug.

4 Pour the mixture into the serving dish and bake in the oven for 20–30 minutes until the custard is just set. (Tap the dish lightly – the custard should wobble seductively!) Leave to cool completely, then chill for at least 4 hours.

5 To serve, preheat the grill to medium. Scatter the demerara sugar over the chilled custard in an even layer, then grill for 2–3 minutes until the sugar has dissolved and caramelised. Cool and chill for 10 minutes before serving.

SAVE TIME

To get ahead, complete the recipe to the end of step 4 up to one day in advance and chill. Complete the recipe to serve.

Serves 2

Use Your Microwave to the Max

Having the right equipment can make life so much easier in the kitchen.
If you have room for a microwave, it's energy-efficient, quick and easy to use –
the busy cook's perfect kitchen companion.

How does it work?

A conventional microwave oven cooks by microwaves that pass through glass, paper, china and plastic and are absorbed by moisture molecules in the food. They penetrate the food to a depth of about 5cm (2in), where they cause the molecules to vibrate and create heat within the food, which cooks it. The manufacturer's instruction booklet will tell you all you need to know to get the best out of the microwave oven, but here are a few handy tips.

Microwave safety:

- ❑ The oven will work only if the door is closed
- ❑ The door has a special seal to prevent microwaves from escaping
- ❑ Never switch on the microwave when there is nothing inside – the waves will bounce off the walls of the oven and could damage the magnetron (the device that converts electricity into microwaves)
- ❑ Allow sufficient space around the microwave for ventilation through the air vents
- ❑ If using plastic containers, use only microwave-safe plastic – ordinary plastic buckles

What to use a microwave for:

❑ Cooking ready-prepared meals
❑ Reheating foods and drinks
❑ Softening butter and melting chocolate

What not to use a microwave for:

❑ Soufflés
❑ Puff pastry
❑ Breaded or battered foods

Microwave tips:

❑ Consult the manufacturer's handbook before you use the microwave for the first time
❑ Use a plastic trivet so that the microwaves can penetrate the underside of the food
❑ Cover fatty foods such as bacon and sausages with kitchen paper to soak up any fat
❑ Stir liquids at intervals during microwaving
❑ Turn large items of food over during microwaving
❑ Clean the interior regularly

Five-minute Microwave Chocolate Pudding

Hands-on time: about 3 minutes
Cooking time: about 1 minute

2½ tbsp cocoa powder

2 tbsp golden syrup

6 tbsp self-raising flour

2½ tbsp caster sugar

1 medium egg

1½ tbsp mild oil

1½ tbsp milk

40g (1½oz) white chocolate, finely chopped

1 Divide 1 tbsp of the cocoa powder equally between two standard mugs. Add 1 tbsp golden syrup to each and mix to a paste. Put the flour, sugar and remaining cocoa powder into a medium bowl. Crack in the egg, add the oil and milk and mix well, then stir in the chocolate.

2 Divide the mixture equally and tidily between the mugs, then cook on full power in an 800W microwave oven for 1 minute 10 seconds. Carefully turn out on to a plate and serve.

Serves 2

Double Chocolate Velvet

Hands-on time: 5 minutes

2 tbsp chocolate syrup
225ml (8fl oz) low-fat chocolate-
    flavoured milk, chilled
100ml (3½fl oz) single cream, chilled
2 scoops chocolate ice cream
2 tbsp dark chocolate sauce
1 milk chocolate flake bar, crushed
a few ice cubes

1 Spoon the syrup into a blender
  and pour in the chocolate milk
  and cream, then add the ice cream.
  Blend until smooth and well mixed.
2 Divide between two tall glasses and
  swirl in the chocolate sauce and half
  the chocolate flake bar.
3 Top up with ice and serve
  immediately, sprinkled with the
  remaining chocolate flake bar.

Chocolate Box

Hands-on time: 10 minutes, plus freezing
Cooking time: about 1 minute

50g (2oz) white chocolate, chopped
50g (2oz) milk chocolate, chopped
50g (2oz) plain chocolate, chopped
a selection of sprinkles, coloured
   sugar, gold leaf and sugar roses to
   decorate

1 Put each type of chocolate into a small, microwave-safe bowl. Put the bowls side by side in the microwave and heat on full power for 1 minute. Continue heating for 10-second bursts until the chocolates are melted and smooth (you may need to take them out at different times).

2 Meanwhile, line two baking sheets with baking parchment. Drop scant teaspoonfuls of the different types of melted chocolate on to the prepared sheets, spacing a little apart, then smooth into rounds with the back of a teaspoon.

3 Decorate the chocolates with sprinkles, coloured sugar, gold leaf or sugar roses. Freeze for 10 minutes to set, then pack into a tissue-lined box. Serve with coffee.

Makes about 36

Sultana and Pecan Cookies

🍴 **Hands-on time:** 15 minutes
Cooking time: about 15 minutes, plus cooling

225g (8oz) unsalted butter, at room
   temperature, plus extra to grease
175g (6oz) light muscovado sugar
2 medium eggs, lightly beaten
225g (8oz) pecan nut halves
300g (11oz) self-raising flour, sifted
¼ tsp baking powder
125g (4oz) sultanas
2 tbsp maple syrup

1 Preheat the oven to 190°C (170°C fan oven) mark 5. Lightly grease four baking sheets.

2 Cream the butter and sugar together until the mixture is pale and fluffy. Gradually beat in the eggs until thoroughly combined.

3 Put 20 pecan nut halves to one side, then roughly chop the rest and fold into the mixture with the flour, baking powder, sultanas and syrup.

4 Roll the mixture into 20 balls and place them, spaced well apart, on the prepared baking sheets. Using a dampened palette knife, flatten the cookies and top each with a piece of pecan nut.

5 Bake for 12–15 minutes until pale golden. Leave on the baking sheets for 5 minutes, then transfer to a wire rack and leave to cool completely. Store in an airtight container. They will keep for up to one week.

FREEZE AHEAD

To make ahead and freeze, complete the recipe to the end of step 4, then open-freeze a tray of unbaked cookies. When frozen, pack into bags or containers. To use, cook from frozen for 18–20 minutes.

Makes 20

Blueberry Muffins

Hands-on time: 10 minutes
Cooking time: about 25 minutes, plus cooling

2 medium eggs
250ml (9fl oz) semi-skimmed milk
250g (9oz) golden granulated sugar
2 tsp vanilla extract
350g (12oz) plain flour
4 tsp baking powder
250g (9oz) blueberries, frozen
finely grated zest of 2 lemons

1 Preheat the oven to 200°C (180°C fan oven) mark 6. Line a 12-hole muffin tin with paper muffin cases.
2 Put the eggs, milk, sugar and vanilla extract into a bowl and mix well.
3 Sift the flour and baking powder together into another bowl, then add the blueberries and lemon zest. Toss together and make a well in the centre.
4 Pour the egg mixture into the flour and blueberries and mix in gently – over-beating will make the muffins tough. Spoon the mixture equally into the paper cases.
5 Bake for 20–25 minutes until risen and just firm. Transfer to a wire rack and leave to cool completely. These muffins are best eaten on the day they are made.

FREEZE AHEAD
Complete the recipe, then pack, seal and freeze the cold muffins. Thaw at cool room temperature to use.

Makes 12

Spiced Carrot Muffins

Hands-on time: 30 minutes
Cooking time: about 25 minutes, plus cooling

125g (4oz) unsalted butter, softened
125g (4oz) light muscovado sugar
3 pieces preserved stem ginger, drained and chopped
150g (5oz) self-raising flour, sifted
1½ tsp baking powder
1 tbsp ground mixed spice
25g (1oz) ground almonds
3 medium eggs
finely grated zest of ½ orange
150g (5oz) carrots, peeled and grated
50g (2oz) pecan nuts, chopped
50g (2oz) sultanas
3 tbsp white rum or orange liqueur (optional)

For the topping and decoration
200g (7oz) cream cheese
75g (3oz) icing sugar
1 tsp lemon juice
12 unsprayed rose petals (optional)

1 Preheat the oven to 180°C (160°C fan oven) mark 4. Line a 12-hole bun tin or muffin tin with paper muffin cases.
2 Beat the butter, muscovado sugar and stem ginger together until pale and creamy. Add the flour, baking powder, spice, ground almonds, eggs and orange zest and beat well until combined. Stir in the carrots, pecan nuts and sultanas. Divide the mixture equally among the paper cases.
3 Bake for 20–25 minutes until risen and just firm. A skewer inserted into the centre should come out clean.

FREEZE AHEAD
To make ahead and freeze, complete the recipe to the end of step 3. Once the muffins are cold, pack, seal and freeze. To use, thaw at cool room temperature and complete the recipe.

Makes 12

Transfer to a wire rack and leave to cool completely.

4 For the topping, beat the cream cheese in a bowl until softened. Beat in the icing sugar and lemon juice to give a smooth icing that just holds its shape.

5 Drizzle each cake with a little liqueur, if you like. Using a small palette knife, spread a little icing over each cake. Decorate with a rose petal, if you like. Store in an airtight container. They will keep for up to one week.

Smoothies and Cocktails

Perfect Smoothies

Fruit, whether cooked or raw, can be transformed into a smooth sauce by puréeing. It also makes a healthy breakfast or snack that is bursting with flavour when used in a smoothie.

Making smoothies

Making your own smoothies can easily become part of your daily routine. All you need to get started is a blender.

A blender is designed to liquidise or 'pulp' whatever is put into it by 'shredding' at a high speed. Free-standing 'jug' blenders have a large removable jug made from glass or sturdy plastic, with metal blades, set on a motor with variable speeds – more expensive models have a blade which is strong enough to crush ice. Never assume that your blender can crush ice, always check the manufacturer's information, otherwise you may seriously damage the motor.

Some food processors have a blender attachment, which fits alongside or on top of the main processing bowl. There are also smaller hand-held blenders, which either come with a small canister or bowl or can be used with your own jug or container. It's worth investigating how the bits and pieces come apart for ease of cleaning and maintenance, and do check that the parts are dishwasher-safe.

Puréeing in a blender

Some fruit can be puréed raw, while others are better cooked. Wait until cooked fruit cools.

1   Blend a spoonful of fruit until smooth, then add another spoonful and blend. Add the rest of the fruit in batches.

2   For a very smooth purée, pass through a fine sieve.

Breakfast Smoothie

Hands-on time: 5 minutes

200ml (7fl oz) semi-skimmed milk

200g (7oz) natural yogurt

125g (4oz) mix of frozen berries, such as blackberries, blueberries and blackcurrants

15g (½oz) rolled oats

2 tbsp runny honey

1 Put all the ingredients into a blender and whiz until smooth. Pour into two tall glasses and serve.

SAVE TIME

If you prefer to have your breakfast ready to go, make a double smoothie batch in the evening, then transfer the mixture to a jug, cover and chill for up to two days. Simply stir before serving.

Serves 2

Apricot and Orange Smoothie

🍴 **Hands-on time:** 5 minutes, plus chilling

400g (14oz) canned apricots in
   natural juice

150g (5oz) apricot yogurt

200–250ml (7–9fl oz) unsweetened
   orange juice

1 Put the apricots, yogurt and
orange juice into a blender or food
processor and whiz for 1 minute or
until smooth.

2 Chill well, then pour into two glasses
and serve.

Cranberry and Mango Smoothie

Hands-on time: 5 minutes

1 ripe mango, stoned
250ml (9fl oz) cranberry juice
150g (5oz) natural yogurt

1 Peel and roughly chop the mango and put into a blender with the cranberry juice. Blend for 1 minute.
2 Add the yogurt and blend until smooth, then serve.

HEALTHY TIP

If you're on a dairy-free diet or are looking for an alternative to milk-based products, swap the yogurt for soya yogurt. Soya is a good source of essential omega-3 and omega-6 fatty acids, and can help to lower cholesterol.

Serves 2

Mango and Oat Smoothie

Hands-on time: 5 minutes

150g (5oz) natural yogurt
1 small mango, peeled, stoned
   and chopped
2 tbsp oats
4 ice cubes

1 Put the yogurt into a blender. Put a little chopped mango to one side for the decoration, if you like, and add the remaining mango, oats and ice cubes to the yogurt. Whiz the ingredients until smooth. Serve immediately, decorated with the chopped mango.

SAVE EFFORT

If you can't find a mango, use 2 nectarines or peaches, or 175g (6oz) soft seasonal fruits such as raspberries, strawberries or blueberries instead.

Serves 2

Perfect Smoothie Boosts

There are many ingredients that you can add to smoothies if you have specific nutritional requirements.

Acidophilus

A probiotic: 'friendly' bacteria that promote good health. Acidophilus is most beneficial when taken if you are suffering from diarrhoea or after a course of antibiotics, or if you have digestive problems such as irritable bowel syndrome (IBS). Available from most chemists and health shops in capsule form, which usually need to be kept in the fridge. Probiotics are now included in some ready-made drinks and yogurt products.

Bee pollen

A natural antibiotic and a source of antioxidants, bee pollen is a good general tonic. It contains plenty of protein and essential amino acids. Available as loose powder, granules or in tablet form.
Warning: it can cause an allergic reaction in pollen-sensitive individuals.

Brewers' yeast

A by-product of beer brewing, brewers' yeast is exceptionally rich in B vitamins, with high levels of iron, zinc, magnesium and potassium. Highly concentrated and an excellent pick-me-up, but the flavour is strong and needs to be mixed with other ingredients. Available as pills or powder.
Warning: is high in purines and so should be avoided by gout sufferers.

Echinacea

Recommended by herbalists for many years, echinacea is a native plant of North America, taken to support a healthy immune system. A great all-rounder with anti-viral and antibacterial properties. Comes in capsules and in extracts taken in drops, so is easy to add to smoothies.
Warning: not recommended for use during pregnancy or when breastfeeding.

Eggs

High in protein, but eggs also contain cholesterol so you might need to limit your intake; ask your GP. Egg white powder is low in fat and can be added to smoothies for a protein boost. Always use the freshest eggs for smoothies.
Warning: raw egg should not be eaten by the elderly, children, babies, pregnant women or those with an impaired immune system, as there can be a risk of contracting salmonella.

Ginseng

Derived from the roots of a plant grown in Russia, Korea and China. The active constituents are ginsenosides, reputed to stimulate the hormones and increase energy. Available in dry root form for grinding or ready powdered.
Warning: should not be taken by those suffering from hypertension.

Nuts

Packed with nutrients, nuts are a concentrated form of protein and are rich in antioxidants, vitamins B1, B6 and E, and many minerals. Brazil nuts are one of the best sources of selenium in the diet. Nuts do have a high fat content, but this is mostly unsaturated fat. Walnuts are particularly high in omega-3, an essential fatty acid that is needed for healthy heart and brain function. Brazil, cashew, coconut, peanut and macadamia nuts contain more saturated fat, so should be used sparingly. Almonds are particularly easy to digest. Finely chop or grind the nuts just before using for maximum freshness.

Seeds

Highly nutritious, seeds contain a good supply of essential fatty acids (EFAs). Flaxseed (linseed) is particularly beneficial as it is one of the richest sources of omega-3 EFAs, with 57% more than oily fish. Pumpkin, sesame and sunflower seeds also work well in smoothies. They are best bought in small amounts as their fat content makes them go rancid quickly, so store in airtight containers in the fridge. Grind them just before use for maximum benefit, or use the oils – these have to be stored in the fridge.

Sprouting seeds

These are simply seeds from a variety of plants – such as sunflower, chickpea and mung bean – which have been given a little water and warmth and have started to grow. Sprouts are full of vitamins, minerals, proteins and carbohydrates. They are pretty soft so they whiz up easily in the blender for savoury smoothies.

Oats

Sold in the form of whole grain, rolled, flaked or ground (oatmeal), oats are high in protein, vitamin B complex, vitamin E, potassium, calcium, phosphorus, iron and zinc; they are easy to digest and can soothe the digestive tract. They are also a rich source of soluble fibre, which helps to lower high blood cholesterol levels, which in turn will help reduce the risk of heart disease. Toasted oatmeal has a nutty flavour and is ideal for smoothies.

Warning: oats should be avoided by those on a gluten-free diet.

Wheat bran and germ

Wheat bran is the outside of the wheat grain removed during milling; it is very high in fibre and adds bulk to the diet. It is bland in taste but adds a crunchy texture. Wheat germ, from the centre of the grain, is very nutritious and easy to digest, with a mild flavour. Highly perishable, store in the fridge once the pack is opened.

Warning: keep your intake of bran to moderate levels; large amounts can prevent vitamins and minerals from being absorbed.

Non-dairy alternatives
Soya milk and yogurt

If you are allergic to dairy products or lactose-intolerant, drinking milk may cause a variety of symptoms, including skin rashes and eczema, asthma and IBS. Soya milk and yogurt are useful alternatives – look for calcium-enriched products. Good non-dairy sources of calcium suitable for adding to smoothies include dark green leafy vegetables, such as watercress and spinach, and apricots.

Silken tofu

This protein-rich dairy-free product adds a creamy texture to fruit and vegetable smoothies.

Busy Bee's Comforter

🍴 **Hands-on time:** 5 minutes

2 lemons
150g (5oz) full-fat natural or soya
   yogurt, at room temperature
1–2 tsp thick honey
2–3 tsp bee pollen grains or equivalent
   in capsule form

1 Using a sharp knife, cut off the peel from one lemon, removing as much of the white pith as possible. Chop the flesh roughly, discarding any pips, and put into a blender. Squeeze the juice from the remaining lemon and add to the blender.

2 Spoon in the yogurt and whiz until smooth. Taste and sweeten with honey as necessary. Stir in the bee pollen, then pour into a glass and serve immediately.

HEALTHY TIP

This drink is a very good source of protein and calcium. It contains honey, which is a source of slow-releasing sugars, and a powerful antibacterial and anti-viral ingredient.
Note: this drink is unsuitable for those with an allergy to pollen, such as hay fever sufferers.

Raspberry Rascal Booster

🍴 **Hands-on time:** 5 minutes

225g (8oz) raspberries, thawed if frozen, juices put to one side

1 medium orange

2 tsp thick honey

1 If using fresh raspberries, remove the hulls, then wash and pat the fruit dry with kitchen paper. Put two raspberries to one side for the decoration and put the rest into a blender. If the fruit has been frozen, add the juices as well.

2 Peel the orange, removing as much of the white pith as possible. Chop the flesh roughly, discarding any pips, and put into the blender. Add the honey. Whiz until smooth, then pour into a glass, decorate with the raspberries and serve immediately.

HEALTHY TIP

This refreshing drink is bursting with vitamin C and anthocyanins, which can help to strengthen blood vessels and boost your immune system.

Serves 1

Fruity Carrot with Ginger

🍴 **Hands-on time:** 10 minutes

2 medium oranges

1cm (½in) piece fresh root ginger, peeled and roughly chopped

150ml (¼ pint) freshly pressed apple juice or 2 dessert apples, juiced

150ml (¼ pint) freshly pressed carrot juice or 3 medium carrots, 250g (9oz), juiced

mint leaves to decorate

1 Using a sharp knife, cut a slice of orange and put to one side for the decoration. Cut off the peel from the oranges, removing as much of the white pith as possible. Chop the flesh roughly, discarding any pips, and put into a blender. Add the ginger.

2 Pour in the apple and carrot juice and blend until smooth. Divide between two glasses, decorate with quartered orange slices and a mint leaf and serve.

HEALTHY TIP

This drink is full of vitamin C and betacarotene, an antioxidant that helps combat harmful free radicals and promotes healthy skin), making it a great immunity-boosting supplement. Fresh ginger is good for calming an upset stomach and providing relief from bloating and gas.

Serves 2

Perfect Cocktails

Brandy Alexander

Hands-on time: 2 minutes

Serves 1

25ml (1fl oz) brandy

25ml (1fl oz) crème de caçao

25ml (1fl oz) double cream

a pinch of grated nutmeg

1 Mix together the brandy, crème de caçao and cream and shake well.

2 Pour into a glass, dust with a little nutmeg and serve.

Variation

For an easy, delicious variation, try a Gin Alexander: just replace the brandy with gin.

Margarita

Hands-on time: 2 minutes

Serves 1

lemon juice

salt

125ml (4fl oz) tequila

25ml (1fl oz) curaçao

25ml (1fl oz) lemon or lime juice

1 Dip the edges of a chilled glass into lemon juice and then salt.

2 Mix the tequila, curaçao and lemon or lime juice in a shaker.

3 Strain into the chilled glass and serve immediately.

Whisky Sour

Hands-on time: 2 minutes
Serves 1

juice of ½ lemon
1 tsp caster sugar
25ml (1fl oz) rye whisky
crushed ice

1 Mix together the lemon juice, sugar and whisky and shake well with the ice.
1 Serve in a whisky tumbler.

Dry Martini

Hands-on time: 2 minutes
Serves 1

50ml (2fl oz) French vermouth
25ml (1fl oz) dry gin
crushed ice
1 stuffed olive or lemon zest curl

1 Shake the vermouth and gin together with some crushed ice in a shaker.
2 Pour into a glass and float an olive or a lemon zest curl on top.

The proportions of a martini are a matter of personal taste; some people prefer 50ml (2fl oz) gin to 25ml (1fl oz) vermouth, others equal quantities of gin and vermouth.

Variation

For an easy, delicious variation, try a Sweet Martini Cocktail: follow the recipe above, but use sweet vermouth and decorate with a cocktail cherry.

Daiquiri

Hands-on time: 2 minutes
Serves 1

juice of ½ lime or ¼ lemon plus extra to serve
1 tsp caster sugar plus extra to frost
25ml (1fl oz) white rum
crushed ice

1 Mix the fruit juice, sugar and rum and shake well with the crushed ice in a shaker.
2 Dip the edges of the glass in a little more fruit juice and then into caster sugar to frost the rim before filling.

Pink Gin

Serves 1

Preparation 2 minutes

2–3 drops Angostura bitters
25ml (1fl oz) gin
50–75ml (2–2½fl oz) iced water

1 Put the bitters into a glass and turn it until the side is well coated.
2 Add the gin and top up with iced water to taste.

Buck's Fizz

Serves 1

Preparation 2 minutes

juice from 1 small orange
150ml (½ pint) champagne

1 Strain the orange juice into a champagne flute and top up with chilled champagne. Serve at once.

Pina Colada

Serves 1

Preparation 2 minutes

85ml (3fl oz) white rum
125ml (4fl oz) pineapple juice
50ml (2fl oz) coconut cream
crushed ice
1 pineapple slice and 1 cherry to decorate

1 Blend together the rum, pineapple juice, coconut cream and crushed ice.
2 Pour into a large goblet or a hollowed-out pineapple half.
3 Decorate with a slice of pineapple and a cherry. Serve with straws.

Irish or Gaelic Coffee

Serves 1

Preparation 5 minutes, plus standing

25ml (1fl oz) Irish whiskey
1 tsp brown sugar
85–125ml (3–4fl oz) hot double-strength coffee
1–2 tbsp double cream, chilled

1 Gently warm a glass, pour in the whiskey and add the brown sugar.
2 Pour in black coffee to within 2.5cm (1in) of the brim and stir to dissolve the sugar.
3 Fill to the brim with cream, poured over the back of a spoon, and allow to stand for a few minutes.

Variations
Liqueur Coffee Around the World
The following are made as for Irish Coffee.

Allow 25ml (1fl oz) of the liqueur or spirit to 125ml (4fl oz) of double-strength black coffee, with sugar to taste – usually about 1 tsp – and some thick double cream to pour on top; these quantities will make 1 glassful:

- **Cointreau Coffee**
  (made with Cointreau)
- **Caribbean Coffee**
  (made with rum)
- **German Coffee**
  (made with Kirsch)
- **Normandy Coffee**
  (made with Calvados)
- **Russian Coffee**
  (made with vodka)
- **Calypso Coffee**
  (made with Tia Maria)
- **Witch's Coffee**
  (made with strega; sprinkle a little grated lemon zest on top)
- **Curaçao Coffee**
  (made with curaçao; stir with a stick of cinnamon)

Egg Nog
Serves 1
Preparation 5 minutes
Cooking time 3 minutes

1 medium egg
1 tbsp sugar
50ml (2fl oz) sherry or brandy
300ml (½ pint) milk

1 Whisk the egg and sugar and add the sherry or brandy.
2 Heat the milk without boiling and pour it over the egg mixture. Stir well and serve hot in a glass.

Bloody Mary

Hands-on time: 2 minutes

1 tbsp Worcestershire sauce
1 dash Tabasco
1 measure (25ml/1fl oz) vodka, chilled
150ml (¼ pint) tomato juice, chilled
ice cubes
lemon juice to taste
celery salt to taste
1 celery stick, with the leaves left on,
   to serve

1 Pour the Worcestershire sauce,
  Tabasco, vodka and tomato juice
  into a tall glass and stir.
2 Add ice cubes and the lemon juice
  and celery salt to taste. Put the
  celery stick in the glass and serve.

Serves 1

Calorie Gallery

343 cal ♥ 23g protein
28g fat (10g sat) ♥ 1g fibre
0.1g carb ♥ 0.9g salt

10

321 cal ♥ 16g protein
25g fat (11g sat) ♥ 1g fibre
0.5g carb ♥ 0.4g salt

12

584 cal ♥ 42g protein
41g fat (23g sat) ♥ 0.1g fibre
11g carb ♥ 3.3g salt

14

246 cal ♥ 30g protein
8g fat (1g sat) ♥ 2g fib
15g carb ♥ 0.6g salt

16

553 cal ♥ 31g protein
27g fat (9g sat) ♥ 4g fibre
50g carb ♥ 0.8g salt

36

496 cal ♥ 15g protein
34g fat (8g sat) ♥ 1g fibre
35g carb ♥ 1.3g salt

38

113 cal ♥ 12g protein
6g fat (1g sat) ♥ 0g fibre
1g carb ♥ 0.1g salt

40

551 cal ♥ 32g protein
35g fat (22g sat) ♥ 1g fibre
27g carb ♥ 3.6g salt

54

317 cal ♥ 18g protein
19g fat (8g sat) ♥ 4g fibre
18g carb ♥ 3.5g salt

56

835 cal ♥ 29g protein
79g fat (46g sat) ♥ 0g fibre
carb 1g ♥ 2.8g salt

58

417 cal ♥ 10g protein
7g fat (1g sat) ♥ 3g fibre
61g carb ♥ 2.9g salt

68

279 cal ♥ 29g protein
15g fat (3g sat) ♥ 3g fibre
7g carb ♥ 0.4g salt

72

170 cal ♥ 21g protein
7g fat (1g sat) ♥ 3g fibre
11g carb ♥ 1.6g salt

74

200 cal ♥ 6g protein
10g fat (2g sat) ♥ 5g fibre
19g carb ♥ 0.7g salt

78

403 cal ♥ 16g protein
g fat (16g sat) ♥ 0g fibre
2g carb ♥ 3.5g salt

without cheese
70 cal ♥ 0.9g protein
6g fat (1g sat) ♥ 3g fibre
2g carb ♥ 0g salt

625 cal ♥ 38g protein
28g fat (8g sat) ♥ 4g fibre
42g carb ♥ 0.4g salt

570 cal ♥ 47g protein
26g fat (8g sat) ♥ 2g fibre
33g carb ♥ 1.2g salt

314 cal ♥ 19g protein
g fat (1g sat) ♥ 21g fibre
44g carb ♥ 3.3g salt

385 cal ♥ 42g protein
13g fat (3g sat) ♥ 6g fibre
26g carb ♥ 0.6g salt

197 cal ♥ 14g protein
16g fat (4g sat) ♥ 7g fibre
5g carb ♥ 1.3g salt

356 cal ♥ 10g protein
27g fat (8g sat) ♥ 3g fibre
21g carb ♥ 2.5g salt

847 cal ♥ 34g protein
51g fat (6g sat) ♥ 4g fibre
67g carb ♥ 1.6g salt

238 cal ♥ 12g protein
1g fat (5g sat) ♥ 3g fibre
2g carb ♥ 0.6g salt

571 cal ♥ 25g protein
31g fat (8g sat) ♥ 3g fibre
57g carb ♥ 2.6g salt

630 cal ♥ 21g protein
28g fat (15g sat) ♥ 3g fibre
77g carb ♥ 1g salt

205 cal ♥ 29g protein
g fat (1g sat) ♥ 0.8g fibre
12g carb ♥ 0.4g salt

308 cal ♥ 22g protein
19g fat (16g sat) ♥ 8g fibre
14g carb ♥ 1g salt

363 cal ♥ 11g protein
32g fat (15g sat) ♥ 0g fibre
0.1g carb ♥ 2.2g salt

382 cal ♥ 18g protein
34g fat (5g sat) ♥ 0g fibre
2g carb ♥ 1.4g salt

180 cal ♥ 19g protein
8g fat (1g sat) ♥ 0.3g fibre
5g carb ♥ 1.1g salt

92

259 cal ♥ 43g protein
9g fat (0g sat) ♥ 0.9g fibre
2g carb ♥ 1.1g salt

94

508 cal ♥ 45g protein ♥
17g fat (4g sat) ♥ 4g fibre ♥
48g carb ♥ 5.1g salt

96

606 cal ♥ 30g protein
32g fat (12g sat) ♥ 6g fib
57g carb ♥ 1.7g salt

98

Calorie Gallery

119 cal ♥ 0.4g protein
0g fat (0g sat) ♥ 0g fibre
16g carb ♥ 0g salt

114

377 cal ♥ 7g protein
21g fat (13g sat) ♥ 0.3g fibre
43g carb ♥ 0.3g salt

118

188 cal ♥ 4g protein
7g fat (1g sat) ♥ 3g fibre
29g carb ♥ 0.2g salt

120

515 cal ♥ 9g protein
30g fat (15g sat) ♥ 0.3g fibre
53.6g carb ♥ 0.4g salt

132

per chocolate: 22 cal
0.3g protein ♥ 1.2g fat
(0.7g sat) ♥ 0.1g fibre
3g carb ♥ 0g salt

134

per cookie: 276 cal
4g protein ♥ 18g fat
(7g sat) ♥ 1.5g fibre
27g carb ♥ 0.2g salt

136

133 cal ♥ 4g protein
1g fat (trace sat) ♥ 2g fibre
29g carb ♥ 0.2g salt

150

145 cal ♥ 6g protein
2g fat (1g sat) ♥ 3g fibre
27g carb ♥ 0.2g salt

152

130 cal ♥ 9g protein
2g fat (1g sat) ♥ 1g fibre
24g carb ♥ 0.3g salt

158

147 cal ♥ 5g protein
1g fat (trace sat) ♥ 8g fibre
39g carb ♥ 0.2g salt

160

431 cal ♥ 12g protein
g fat (5g sat) ♥ 7g fibre
65g carb ♥ 1.8g salt

227 cal ♥ 14g protein
4g fat (1g sat) ♥ 15g fibre
33g carb ♥ 1.8g salt

370 cal ♥ 27g protein
28g fat (18g sat) ♥ 0g fibre
0.1g carb ♥ 1.9g salt

737 cal ♥ 37g protein
65g fat (40g sat) ♥ 0g fibre
2g carb ♥ 1.7g salt

104

108

112

622 cal ♥ 5g protein
g fat (25g sat) ♥ 0.7g fibre
50g carb ♥ 0.2g salt

447 calories ♥ 5g protein
34g fat (20g sat) ♥ 0g fibre
27g carb ♥ 0.1g salt

516 cal ♥ 10g protein
19g fat (6g sat) ♥ 2g fibre
77g carb ♥ 0.8g Salt

539 cal ♥ 7g protein
48g fat (30g sat) ♥ 0g fibre
22g carb ♥ 0.9g salt
124

126

130

218 cal ♥ 5g protein
fat (trace sat) ♥ 2g fibre
49g carb ♥ 0.5g salt

333 cal ♥ 5g protein
22g fat (11g sat) ♥ 1g fibre
31g carb ♥ 0.5g salt

205 cal ♥ 10g protein
3g fat (2g sat) ♥ 2g fibre
36g carb ♥ 0.3g salt

172 cal ♥ 4g protein
1g fat (trace sat) ♥ 2g fibre
39g carb ♥ 0.2g salt

140

146

148

128 cal ♥ 2g protein
g fat (trace sat) ♥ 5g fibre
30g carb ♥ 0.1g salt

96 cal ♥ 0.3g protein
0g fat ♥ 0.2g fibre
9g carb ♥ 1.8g salt

168

Index

PICTURE CREDITS
Photographers:
Neil Barclay (page 55); Steve Baxter (pages 2, 7 left, 11, 15, 17, 25 left, 25 right, 31, 33, 43, 69, 117 right and 131); Martin Brigdale (pages 45 left, 73 and 75); Nicki Dowey (pages 27, 51, 53, 77 left, 79, 81, 91, 95, 117 left, 121, 123, 125, 133, 137, 139, 141, 142, 143 left, 149, 153, 159, 161, 163 and 169); Will Heap (pages 45 right, 61 and 151); Fiona Kennedy (page 57); William Lingwood (page 111); Gareth Morgans (pages 6, 19, 24, 28, 37, 41, 49, 76 and 85); Myles New (pages 13 and 39); Craig Robertson (pages 8, 34, 35, 44, 63, 70, 71, 83, 89, 107, 110 and 145); Maja Smend (pages 77 right and 99); Sam Stowell (pages 7 right and 21); Lucinda Symons (pages 59, 65, 67, 87, 93 and 97); Kate Whitaker (pages 101, 102, 103 left, 103 right, 105, 109, 113, 115, 116, 119, 127, 135, 143 right and 147).

Home Economists:
Anna Burges-Lumsden, Joanna Farrow, Emma Jane Frost, Teresa Goldfinch, Alice Hart, Lucy McKelvie, Kim Morphew, Aya Nishimura, Katie Rogers, Bridget Sargeson, Stella Sargeson, Kate Trend, Sarah Tildesley, Jennifer White, Mari Mereid Williams.

Stylists:
Susannah Blake, Tamzin Ferdinando, Wei Tang, Sarah Tildesley, Helen Trent, Fanny Ward, Mari Mereid Williams.

BAKE ME A CAKE

There's always time for cake

EASY PEASY MEALS

Easy meals for every day

LET'S DO BRUNCH

Mouth-watering meals to start your day

CHEAP EATS

Budget-busting ideas that won't break the bank

WONDERFUL ONE-POTS

Easy peasy recipes made in just one pot

Available online at store.anovabooks.com and from all good bookshops

SUPER SOUPS

Sumptuous soups for every day

SKINNY SUPPERS

Delicious, nutritious recipes under 300 calories

SLOW STOPPERS

Slow-cooked meals packed with flavour

GREAT VEG

Inspired ideas for delicious veggie meals

AL FRESCO EATS

Easy grills, barbecues and picnics

ROAST IT

There's nothing better than a delicious roast

FLASH IN THE PAN

Spice up your noodles and stir-fries

GLUTEN-FREE AND EASY

Oh-so-good-for-you recipes that taste great

LOW FAT LOW CAL

Nice recipes don't need to be naughty